You have your way.

I have my way.

As for the right way,

the correct way,

and the only way,

it does not exist!

~ Friedrich Nietzsche

The WALK THE TALK Company

Helping organizations and individuals achieve success through
Ethical Leadership and Values-Based Business Practices

GENERATIONS WORKING TOGETHER

Inquiries regarding permission for use of the material contained in this book should be addressed to:
The WALK THE TALK Company
2925 LBJ Freeway, Suite 201
Dallas, Texas 75234
972.243.8863

WALK THE TALK books may be purchased for educational, business, or sales promotion use.

WALK THE TALK® and The WALK THE TALK® Company are registered trademarks of Performance Systems Corporation.

Printed in the United States of America.

10 9 8 7 6 5 4 3 2

Produced and designed by Steve Ventura
Edited by Michelle Sedas
Printed by MultiAd

ISBN 1-885228-70-8

9 781885 228703

90000

GENERATIONS
working together

What Everyone Needs to KNOW and DO!

Laura E. Bernstein

ACKNOWLEDGMENTS

Special thanks to
ERIC HARVEY and **STEVE VENTURA**
and the wonderful teams at
VisionPoint Productions
&
The WALK THE TALK Company
for "working together" with me
to make this book a reality.

INTRODUCTION

*"I HAD the information and she just shut me down.
I'm not some punk kid; I've been doing this for five years."*

**"Nobody wants to hear from the old guy.
When they're not thinking I've lost it,
they're planning my retirement party."**

*"I've been called a 'workaholic,' and I guess
sometimes I expect the same from others."*

"She lives her life to work; I work to have a life."

*"They NEED technology and we KNOW technology.
But it's hard to make the trip when the dinosaurs
won't come along for the ride!"*

Sound familiar?

Perhaps you've thought, said, or heard one (or more) of those phrases – or others like them – recently at work. And if that's the case, your business environment is fairly normal ... and ripe for problems.

You see, besides being laments, those phrases also are natural responses to two characteristics displayed by an ever-growing number of organizations today:

1. People from different generations are working at the same place at the same time – all trying to contribute to the same mission.

In the United States (and many other countries) a new demographic has emerged. For the first time in modern history, **four generations exist in the workplace** in significant numbers. Most organizations *are*, or soon *will be*, encountering "generational diversity" issues in their workforces ... or with their customers, clients, or suppliers.

2. Everyone has different perspectives on the meaning of "employment," how work should be done, and what workplaces should be like – all of which add to the potential for conflict.

Each generation has been significantly shaped by its environment ... by the political, social, and economic climates its members grew up in. Generally speaking, each has distinct values, behaviors, expectations, attitudes, and biases which often clash with each other.

Fact is, ALL organizations today are prone to friction between different generations. And in far too many cases, coworkers lack both the understanding and skills necessary to narrow these classic "generation gaps." That's a huge problem!

Left unchecked, generational differences at work can negatively impact everything from interpersonal relationships, teamwork, morale, and overall productivity – to an organization's ability to recruit and retain top-notch people and achieve its overall mission. When that happens, everyone loses.

But it doesn't have to be that way.

As you read the information that follows, you'll become more familiar with the four generations that comprise today's workforce. You will discover why people of different age groups tend to think, feel, and act as they do. And you'll learn a variety of strategies and techniques for finding "a common ground" for working more effectively, collaboratively, and productively with *everyone* on your team.

The moment you signed on with your organization, you became responsible for treating all coworkers and customers with dignity and respect. The ideas and strategies presented in this book will not only help you meet that responsibility, but also bring many personal benefits as well.

Reduced tension and stress, fewer obstacles, more satisfaction, enhanced respect, and higher levels of success are just a few pluses you can expect – and will have earned – if you APPLY what you read.

So, read on. And as you begin, **make a sincere commitment to put this information to use**. You owe that to your teammates, to your customers, and to your organization.

Most importantly, you owe it to yourself.

CONTENTS

I may not

be *better*

than other people,

but at least

I'm *different*!

~ Jean-Jacques Rousseau

GENERATIONS: THE WHOs, WHATs, and WHYs

Knowledge is the best eraser in the world
for disharmony, distrust, despair,
and the endless deficiencies of man.

~ Orlando Battista

Each of us is a member of a generation – a group of people who experienced (and are bound together by) the same events and similar influences during our formative years. And, of course, we're also members of today's workforce which is comprised of four distinct generations – each with its own label:

LABEL	BORN BETWEEN
"Traditionalists"	1925-1945
"Baby Boomers"	1946-1964
"Generation X"	1965-1981
"Generation Y"	1982-2002

Note: While the specific "born between" dates listed above (and throughout this book) may be debated,
the time frames they represent are generally accepted as accurate for discussion purposes.

Typically, behavioral differences between these four generations are apparent in areas such as clothing preferences and appearance, speech patterns and communication styles, approaches to tasks and assignments, leadership strategies and techniques, the use, allocation, and management of time, and the definitions of *loyalty*, *career*, and even *work* itself.

To be sure, each of us is a unique human being. As such, we do not fit perfectly into any one mold or category. We will not exhibit every characteristic commonly associated with *our* generation. However, it's also true that our individual beliefs, preferences, and values TEND to be aligned with those of our generational counterparts, and often differ from those of other generations. And it's no secret that those differences increase the potential for conflict – all too frequently resulting in:

- ◆ *decreased* productivity, quality, and innovation.
- ◆ *decayed* attitudes, relationships, and working environments.
- ◆ *deprived* customers and shareholders.
- ◆ *destroyed* motivation, initiative, and teamwork.

Those characteristics universally describe a lousy place to work – no matter the specific generational perspective from which they are viewed. Obviously, it's important to ensure that those same negative characteristics don't apply to *our* organizations.

So, the challenge is clear: find ways to work more effectively together. The first step in meeting that challenge: enhance our **knowledge** and **understanding** of why generations are the way they are.

Understanding "Traditionalists"

Born before the end of World War II, this generation is also referred to as "Veterans," "Builders," "Matures," and "The Silent Generation." Although many in this group are at, or past, the age of retirement, they are staying in the workforce longer – reflecting both the need for their skills and the impact of laws prohibiting discrimination based on age. As would be expected, however, the number of working members of this generation will be reduced significantly over the next several years.

Traditionalists are typically characterized by core values such as dedication, honor, loyalty, respect for rules and authority, frugality, self-discipline, and an overall *duty first* approach to life. They tend to be polite, respectful, re-served, and obedient – the least likely of all team members to openly speak their minds, question instructions, abuse privileges, or "make a scene" in public.

With few exceptions, members of this group tend to be **conformers** who view work as an obligation of adulthood rather than a source of fulfillment or self-realization. For them, employment exists for the sole purpose of earning a living ... of "paying your own way" – and it's something that is best man-aged by a command-and-control, military style of leadership.

Traditionalists typically feel that electronic forms of communication are cold and impersonal (not to mention complex and confusing). For them, commu-nication is best done one-on-one – either in person, by phone, or through a personal note. When it comes to receiving feedback, no news usually is good news ("As long as I don't hear from the boss, I'm doing okay"). And often, the only recognition they need and expect, besides being "respected as elders," is the personal satisfaction that comes from a job done well.

Traditionalists are often perceived (i.e., stereotyped) as somewhat rigid, autocratic, and behind in technology.

To understand traditionalist beliefs and behaviors, one needs only to examine the influences of their youth. These are people who grew up in the shadow of the Great Depression. Most were impacted by the horror of Pearl Harbor, the call to arms for both World War II and Korea, and the need to support the war efforts at home. During their formative years, mobility was limited, resources for living were sparse, and the term *technology* pretty much equated to radios and telephones. They were taught to save rather than spend, "make the most of what you have," "do what you're told," and emulate the heroes of the day – many of whom were honored military figures.

A Quick Word on "Cuspers"

Besides "Traditionalists," "Baby Boomers," "Generation X," and "Generation Y," your workforce will also have **"Cuspers"** – those born near the end of one generation or the beginning of the next. People in this category may identify more directly with one of the generations they overlap, but can share the characteristics of either. And they tend to relate well to both of the generations they fall between.

Understanding "Baby Boomers"

Born between 1946 and 1964, Baby Boomers (or "Boomers") have continually shaped and redefined American culture during the past forty to fifty years. Now in their early forties to early sixties, members of this group currently dominate the ranks of senior management in business organizations as well as positions of power in our political institutions. The first wave of aging Boomers is bringing new meaning to the term *old* – and to the concept of *retirement* – for our entire society.

Baby Boomers are typically characterized by core values such as optimism, involvement, respect for power and accomplishment, "paying your dues," team orientation, personal development, and self-gratification. These are **competitors** who believe that success is only achieved through hard work (i.e., long hours) and by "playing nice." For them, work tends to be a source of personal identity and fulfillment – one that is best rewarded with advancement, titles, and the tangible accoutrements (office furniture, parking spaces, etc.) that come with professional achievement.

Often uncomfortable with conflict and autocracy, Boomers typically gravitate to collegial, consensus-building approaches to leadership. They expect a certain level of formality and protocol – since that's how things were when they first started working. They tend to be *social animals* who enjoy human interaction ... as long as it's cooperative and "peaceful" in nature. And even though it hasn't come naturally, most Boomers have developed skills with computers (and other forms of technology) because they know such adeptness is necessary for progress. These are, after all, the people who are willing to give whatever it takes to succeed – the LIVE TO WORK generation.

"The rap" on Baby Boomers is that they tend to be workaholics, politically sensitive (to a fault), idealistic, and lacking any appropriate balance between their jobs and personal lives.

So, why is it that Baby Boomers think and act as they do? A look at the influences of *their* formative years offers several clues.

These are people who grew up in a time of significant scientific advances, dramatic social changes, and the economic prosperity of the post-World War II years. They saw the elimination of the dreaded polio disease, the introduction of birth control pills, and human beings take the first trips into outer space, land on the moon, and return safely to earth. During their youth, the Civil Rights Act was passed, the Peace Corps was established, the National Organization for Women was founded, and Martin Luther King Jr. led the history-making March on Washington.

As children and young adults, they sat in front of their televisions and ex-perienced first-hand the horrors of the Vietnam War, the pain of their heroes being assassinated, and the optimistic resolve of the inspiring words *we shall overcome*. They learned to give all of their effort to what they believe in, to measure themselves by their accomplishments, and – with the advent of convenient credit cards – to "buy now and pay later."

Understanding "Generation X"

Gen Xers – also known as "Baby Busters" and "The 13th Generation" – were born between 1965 and 1981. Now in their middle twenties to early forties, this group has a strong presence in key mid-manager, supervisor, and team leader positions. And many of them are at, or are rapidly approaching, the midpoint of their working careers.

The core values and traits typically associated with Generation X include: self-reliance, results orientation, informality, skepticism, and individualism. These are status quo **challengers** for whom work tends to be more of a "contract" to deliver results in exchange for compensation – rather than a source of identity or fulfillment. One of their key mantras is: *Tell me what you need done and when you need it – but don't tell me how or where to do it.*

Gen Xers are often skeptical of "institutions" – and of leaders who know less, and have accomplished less, than the people who report to them. Their communication style tends to be similar to their work pace: fast, direct, im-mediate, and technology-based. For them, cell phones, laptops, and PDAs are required for maximum efficiency; freedom and flexibility are the best rewards for achievement.

Not prone to working extensive overtime or on weekends, members of this generation tend to reject formality, rules, and protocol – all of which hamper their ability to get the job done quickly so they can leave and get on with their personal lives.

When compared to their predecessors, members of Generation X are occasionally seen as, and criticized for, being impatient, cynical, self-centered, disloyal, and lacking a "traditional" work ethic. To better understand this WORK TO LIVE generation, let's take a brief look at what its members experienced while growing up.

For the most part, Gen Xers were raised in the prosperous, mobile, and fairly materialistic culture created by the previous generation. They have been significantly influenced by shifts in family and societal trends – including divorce, two-income households, and gender, racial, and ethnic diversity. Their ever-working Baby Boomer parents were determined that "our kids are going to have it even better than we did" – often using *presents* to compensate for their lack of *presence*.

Progressing from daycare to staying at home, alone, with electronic babysitters (television, video games, computers, etc.), many members of this generation learned to be independent ... to fend for themselves ... to gravitate toward those things that provide pleasure and immediate satisfaction.

Their skepticism was fueled by events such as the Munich Olympics murders and other terrorist attacks, Watergate, the Tylenol scare, the Three Mile Island and Chernobyl accidents, oil spills, the Challenger disaster, and the Jonestown mass suicide. And the term *loyalty* was debunked and redefined as they watched many hard-working Boomers fall victim to corporate layoffs after years of dedicated service.

Understanding "Generation Y"

Those born between 1982 and 2002 have been given many additional labels, including: "Gen-Next," "Echo Boomers," "Millennials," "the Digital (or Net) Generation," and "the Mosaic Generation." Currently in their early twenties and younger, this group is entering the workforce in significant and ever-increasing numbers. They are expected to eventually become an even larger demographic than Baby Boomers – with an equally distinct and significant impact on society and the workplaces of the future.

The core values and traits typically associated with members of Generation Y include: pragmatism, self-confidence, tenacity, inquisitiveness, extreme informality, and social consciousness. These are task-oriented **technocrats** for whom work tends to be a stepping stone ... a "gig" ... an event ... a necessary way of filling time between weekends ... something that should be FUN to do. As a result, they tend to be the least likely of all generations to put in for promotions, seek out additional responsibilities, or willingly give extra hours to team tasks or projects.

Gen Yers typically work *and play* at "warp speed" – and have great difficulty understanding and accepting tedious rules, protocols, and what they perceive as the overall slower, less efficient pace of their predecessors. They tend to measure time in *nanoseconds*, demand options and choices, and expect attention and feedback. For them, multitasking through multimedia isn't a tool or strategy; it's a way of life – the only one they've really ever known. And, from their perspective, concepts like *commitment*, *tradition*, and *dress codes* are pretty much irrelevant when it comes to "doing the job you hired me to do."

Members of this group are sometimes perceived as spoiled, impatient, ego-centric, and technology dependent.

What were the influences of Generation Y's formative years? Well, clearly, this group has been brought up in one of the most child-centered eras that has ever existed. Raised in a time of seemingly limitless possibilities, they have been nurtured, coddled, pampered, and groomed (a.k.a. "programmed") from their early infancy. They have grown up receiving continual feedback and reinforcement from teachers, coaches, and parents – the majority of whom conveyed the same, consistent messages: *Be the best ... express yourself ... you are special ... you can do more and better ... speak your mind ... be all that you can be.*

For many members of this group, shuttling from soccer practice, to karate class, to dance lessons, to swim meets was the childhood norm – teaching them to "shift gears" quickly and collaborate with fellow team members. As *techno-toddlers*, their early mastery of computers created the expectation of immediacy when it came to acquiring information, communicating with others (globally as well as locally), and even printing their photographs. Because of a myriad of options and choices, finding satisfying (albeit short-lived) entertainment often entailed quickly "surfing" through *hundreds* of TV channels and websites, and scouring bookshelves filled with the latest video games and music downloads.

In general, this group learned to do more, accomplish more, and expect to be *given* more than any previous generation. For many Gen Yers, life is about abundance. And their overall perspectives on work and business have, to a large degree, been shaped by media stories about successful entrepreneurs, workforce layoffs, and corporate scandals.

GENERATIONAL DIFFERENCES IN KEY WORKPLACE DIMENSIONS

	"Traditionalists"	"Baby Boomers"	"Generation X"	"Generation Y"
Work Style	By the book; "How" is as important as what gets done	Get it done; Whatever it takes (including nights and weekends)	Take fastest route to results; Protocol is secondary	Work to deadlines and goals – not necessarily to schedules
Authority / Leadership	Command and control; Rarely question authority	Respect for power and accomplishment	Egalitarian; Rules are flexible; Collaboration is important	Value freedom and autonomy; Less inclined to pursue leadership positions
Communication	Formal yet personal; Through proper channels	Somewhat formal through structured network; Mix of electronic and face-to-face	Casual, direct, and electronic; Sometimes skeptical	Fast, casual, direct, and high-tech; Eager to please
Recognition / Reward	Personal acknowledgment and satisfaction for work done well	Public acknowledgment and career advancement	A balance of fair compensation and ample time off	Individual and public praise (exposure); Opportunities for broadening skills
Work / Family	Work and family should be kept separate	Work comes first	Value a work / life balance	Value blending personal life into work
Loyalty	To the ORGANIZATION	To the importance and meaning of work; To the function or profession	To individual career goals	To the people involved with the project
Technology	Complex and challenging; "If it ain't broke, don't fix it"	Necessary for progress and achievement	Practical tools for getting things done	What else is there?

WORDS TO REMEMBER

Intolerance has been the curse of every age and state.
~ Samuel Davies

*The shoe that fits one person pinches another;
there is no recipe for living that suits all cases.*
~ Carl Jung

The real death of America will come when everyone is alike.
~ James T. Ellison

*You never really understand a person until you
consider things from his [or her] point of view.*
~ Harper Lee

*We need to remember across generations that
there is as much to learn as there is to teach.*
~ Gloria Steinem

It takes all sorts to make a world.
~ English Proverb

We all have the same dreams.
~ Joan Didion

NARROWING THE GENERATION GAPS

Unity, not uniformity, must be our aim.
We attain unity only through variety.
Differences must be integrated,
not annihilated, not absorbed.

~ Mary Parker Follett

It's a fact: The better that people from different generational groups are able to work together effectively, the more satisfying and productive the workplace will be. And that fact naturally leads to a critical question ... to *the* question:

What can you do to narrow the gaps that
inherently exist between generations?

The answer lies within (and through) the following five "**A** list" strategies:

1. **A**ccepting your "mutual rightness."
2. **A**cknowledging your interdependency.
3. **A**ppreciating what you have in common.
4. **A**ssuming responsibility for making your relationships better.
5. **A**dopting "The Platinum Rule."

Accepting Your "Mutual Rightness"

As humans, our values and perspectives are shaped by the myriad of people, experiences, environments, and events we encounter during our formative years (our *youth*). We're all natural "products of our times." And as such, with very few exceptions, each of us is normal ... each of us is RIGHT – regardless of how we may vary from others.

Certainly, there are times when differing viewpoints are unacceptable. Take, for example, the small handful of people who believe it's perfectly okay to lie, cheat, steal, and disrespect their way to success. No matter how you cut it, those folks are just plain wrong and should not be tolerated, much less condoned. But, we all know that they are the extreme exception rather than the general rule. For the most part, being "different" does not make you wrong – it just makes you different. And that's something all of us need to come to grips with and accept.

Just as your beliefs are appropriate and correct *for you*, coworkers who don't share your views have beliefs, mindsets, and attitudes that are equally appropriate and correct ... *for them*. Ignore this fact – label them WRONG – and you'll self-righteously presume that they need to change (and stubbornly wait for them to do it). But acknowledge and accept that they are as right as you are, and you're more likely to pursue more respectful and collaborative ways of working together through which everyone wins.

No two people are exactly the same. So, if being different was to equal being wrong, EVERYONE would be wrong – including YOU!

~ Steve Ventura, *Start Right ... Stay Right*

Acknowledging Your Interdependency

Pretend for a moment that you were assigned the task of creating a blueprint for the perfect employee ... "the total package." What would that person be like? What knowledge, skills, and experiences would he or she possess?

Chances are, your ideal team member would be a technology wizard, a historian, a politician, and a "go-to player." He or she probably would be **PC** savvy (**P**ersonal **C**omputing *and* **P**olitical **C**orrectness). This would be a person adept at every professional discipline – from finance, planning, and design, to marketing, sales, and production. Your blueprint would likely include equal parts of logic and emotion, drive and restraint, protocol and informality, tradition and innovation, knowledge of what's been done in the past along with the ability to not be hampered by it, detail focus and big-picture orientation, and both "in the box" and "off the wall" thinking. YES, your perfect employee would be a composite of all the factors and attributes your business needs in order to be successful. And NO, that person does not exist!

Fact is, no single person – or single *type* of person – can provide everything a business (and its employees) needs to prosper in today's global economy. That's why we have teams ... why we form organizations. Because we are **interdependent**, we *need* coworkers who think and act differently than ourselves – people who bring diverse skills, abilities, and perspectives to the table. YOU need them ... and they need you!

Keep that in mind and it is likely that you'll not only approach interactions in a more collaborative fashion, but also look for ways to contribute to each other's success.

Appreciating What You Have in Common

Have you ever looked at a coworker from another generation and thought: *He (or she) and I are as different as night and day. We have absolutely NOTHING in common!* If you answered "yes," several things are pretty much true: you're truly honest, you're very normal, and you need to do some serious rethinking.

Why rethinking? Because you're undoubtedly a lot more similar to others than your emotions are leading you to believe. Want proof? Think of that same coworker (referenced above) who you feel is so completely different from you. Lock his or her image in your mind. Now, imagine you're given a pad, a pencil, and the following assignment: "You have one hour to make a list of all the things you and that person have in common. You'll be given a one-hundred dollar bill for every item on your list." What do you suppose would happen? There's a good chance that your list would be jam-packed with personal similarities. Sure, you probably would have written down a bunch of physical (anatomical) matches such as: two eyes, two arms, one mouth, etc. But if your list had some real thinking behind it, it would also include things like: *We both work for the same organization ... We both want to be valued and respected ... We both want to contribute in our own ways ... We both want to feel good about ourselves and what we do ... We both want to be successful and make a difference.* And factors such as those should lead you to a logically accurate and powerfully profound conclusion:

WE HAVE MUCH MORE IN COMMON THAN I ORIGINALLY THOUGHT!

Look for and appreciate the similarities that bind you to others – rather than focusing on the differences that divide you. It will make getting along and working together a whole lot easier.

Assuming Responsibility
for Making Your Relationships Better

When it comes to workplace interactions, two truths are undeniable:

1. We *rarely* (if ever) get to choose the people we work with.

2. We *always* get to choose how we deal with and respond to those same coworkers.

Think about it for a moment. If someone at work "gets under your skin," it happens because *you* allow him or her to do so; if you "just can't work with" a fellow team member, for whatever the reason, *you* have made that call; if you have an unaddressed issue with someone and it's hampering cooperation and congeniality, *you* are the one letting it fester.

Granted, relationships are two-way streets ... fifty-fifty propositions requiring *both* parties to work at keeping things positive, productive, and mutually beneficial. But someone needs to set the tone for working together effectively. And if things turn sour, someone needs to take the first step at making them better. That someone must be the one person you have total control over: YOU!

When you assume responsibility for improving the relationships you have with your coworkers, you not only earn the right to expect them to do the same, but also increase the likelihood that they'll meet you halfway. Even if they don't, you will have done *your* part ... you will have done the right thing.

Adopting "The Platinum Rule"

Most people are familiar with the timeless "Golden Rule" – *Treat others the way you would like to be treated.* And while it is truly a wonderful guide to our human interactions, that tenet does have one basic flaw. Since people are unique individuals with varying needs, desires, and perspectives, some folks may not *want* to be dealt with in the exact same manner as you do.

Certainly, like you, everyone else at work expects to be treated fairly – with dignity and respect. We all want to be listened to, to have our ideas and concerns considered, and to feel that we (and our work) truly matter. But *how* we'd like those universal expectations to be met is where we tend to differ. For every person who enjoys public praise, there's someone else who prefers to be recognized privately. For every team member who wants direct and candid feedback, there's another who likes the medicine with a little sugar. For every person who wants to lead, there is someone else who operates best as a committed follower. For every colleague who ... oh well, you get the picture.

Bottom line: There are no clones of you floating around out there. So, rather than treating others the way you want to be treated, consider treating them the way THEY want to be treated. That's called "The Platinum Rule" – and it's one of the very best guides for improving intergenerational relationships.

Think of the people you work with and for. What behaviors do they engage in? How do they tend to get their work done? What seems important to them? What generational characteristics do they exhibit? What are their obvious likes and dislikes? By answering these questions, you'll develop a feel for what makes your colleagues 'tick.' Then, use that information to enhance your daily interactions.

ADDITIONAL TIPS & SUGGESTIONS

DOs and DON'Ts for Working Effectively with *Every* Generation

DO ...

☑ Recognize and accept that generational differences naturally influence our ideas, expectations, values, perceptions, and behaviors at work.

☑ Acknowledge that everyone wants to be treated with dignity and respect. And, remember that based on their individual experiences and perspectives, those expectations will likely be defined differently by different people.

☑ Give coworkers, customers, and suppliers the same "benefit of the doubt" that you wish from them. Presume that the people you interact with are motivated by good and noble intentions – unless they prove otherwise.

☑ Accept that you can learn from others' different life experiences, perspectives, and approaches – just as others can learn from yours.

☑ Make an effort to focus on your similarities with others rather than your differences. Find, appreciate, and celebrate the common ground you share with those you work with ... and work for.

DO ...

☑ Be willing to flex your natural style and preferences in order to work more effectively with all of your colleagues. Continually remind yourself that increased cooperation and collaboration result in greater success for EVERYONE!

☑ Be open and tactfully honest about your personal "hot buttons" (i.e., recurring sources of tension or conflict) and mindful of the things that bother others.

☑ Give your colleagues specific suggestions on what they can do to help you perform at your best. And by all means, ask them to share similar information with you.

☑ Continually challenge your beliefs, opinions, and assumptions about individuals from different generations.

☑ Remember that each individual brings something special (and needed) "to the table" ... each person represents a piece that must be present in order for your organizational puzzle to be complete.

☑ Focus on what really matters: productivity, teamwork, customer service, and mutual success.

☑ Accept the <u>fact</u> that how you treat, deal with, and respond to others is purely and simply a matter of your own choosing.

DON'T ...

○ Stereotype! Avoid judging your colleagues' capabilities by what they wear, how they approach tasks, or what hours they *seem* to work.

○ Ridicule others. Avoid derogatory labels like "dinosaur," "punk kid," "bureaucrat," "antique," "Gramps," "company man / woman," "the establishment," etc., that are disrespectful, degrading, and counterproductive to group cohesion.

○ Assume that all members of any given generation think and behave exactly the same. While trends and similarities will exist within age groups, members of those groups still are INDIVIDUALS and should be treated as such.

○ Entertain the arrogant belief that *your* way is the best and only way — and that those who think and act differently than you are inherently wrong. If you catch yourself falling into that trap, take a moment to reflect on the innovations and successes your team has experienced from diverse people and approaches.

○ Presume that your time, your ideas, your feelings, or your individual goals are more important than those of your colleagues.

○ Think it's okay to succeed and advance yourself at others' expense.

THE VOCABULARY OF
NARROWING GENERATION GAPS

The **10** key words:
  "We have a lot more in common than I thought."

The **9** key words:
  "How can we help each other be more successful?"

The **8** key words:
  "I'd like to share my ideas with you."

The **7** key words:
  "Neither of us can do it alone."

The **6** key words:
  "Please tell me what you're feeling."

The **5** key words:
  "Let's learn from each other."

The **4** key words:
  "What do you think?"

The **3** key words:
  "We're both right."

The **2** key words:
  "Thank you."

The **1** key word:
  ## *"We."*

Tips for Working Effectively With
"TRADITIONALISTS"

SUMMARY OVERVIEW

Born between: 1925-1945
Motto: *Duty first.*
History: Grew up during a time of economic and political uncertainty. Influenced by clearly defined sex roles and the "military model" (structure, protocols, hierarchy, chain of command).
Characteristics: Generally seen as dedicated, loyal, long-term employees. Primary loyalty is to their organization ("I work for ....").

☑ Acknowledge their experience, expertise, dedication, and length of service (if applicable).

☑ Pay attention to the chain of command and its importance to getting things done in certain areas of the organization. Don't circumvent ("go around" or "go over the heads of") these valuable coworkers.

☑ Speak positively of your organization's history – and its legacy that members of this group helped to create.

☑ Demonstrate interest in, and a sense of importance for, the work you're doing (e.g., projects, processes, products, and bottom-line results).

☑ Appreciate and take advantage of the insights they've gained from years of experience. "Pick their brains" and use them as resources when you have questions and problems.

$\bigcirc$ Don't refer to, or make humorous remarks about, their age – even if they do it, themselves. This applies to well-intended compliments as well. Saying something like: *See, you **can** teach old dogs new tricks* may be taken as an insult even though your intention was to compliment the person on his or her willingness to learn and try new approaches.

$\checkmark$ Be patient with their approaches to technology. Members of this generation are the least likely to be "cyber proficient." So, don't look down on them or make them feel bad. Instead, offer your assistance in helping them become more computer savvy and comfortable.

My "Traditionalist" Coworkers
To Whom This Information Applies:
(write names in box)

Tips for Working Effectively With
"BABY BOOMERS"

SUMMARY OVERVIEW

Born between: 1946-1964

Motto: *Anything is possible.*

History: Grew up during a time of economic prosperity and positive change that was viewed as "progress" and that included progressive views on child rearing.

Characteristics: Generally seen as optimistic and competitive. Willing to work long and hard to ensure personal and organizational success. Primary loyalty is to their profession / function ("I'm a ....").

☑ Acknowledge their experience, expertise, dedication, and length of service (if applicable).

☑ Seek their help and counsel with issues involving workplace politics. Observe (and learn) how they navigate politically charged environments and "the system." Use them as mentors.

☑ When communicating with members of this group, strike a balance between e-mails / voice mail (which can be seen as impersonal) and face-to-face conversations / meetings.

☑ Use them as "sounding boards" to test new ideas *before* plunging in. Solicit their perspectives on **what** has worked (or not worked) in the past ... and **why**.

☑ Focus on relationships as well as results. Members of this group tend to value socialization and *the human touch*. So, build in time for informal, nonbusiness conversations. Here, again, you need to strike a balance. This time it's between "small talk" and "cutting to the chase."

☑ Look for ways to demonstrate to these folks that you are carrying your share of the load. Avoid flaunting alternative work schedules or arrangements that apply to you or your coworkers.

My "Baby Boomer" Coworkers
To Whom This Information Applies:
(write names in box)

Tips for Working Effectively With
"GENERATION X"

SUMMARY OVERVIEW

Born between: 1965-1981

Motto: *Achieve a work / life balance.*

History: Grew up during a time of change that negatively impacted family (increasing divorce rate), jobs (massive layoffs), economy (double-digit inflation), public trust (Watergate), and the environment (oil spills, endangered species).

Characteristics: Generally seen as skeptical of authority and institutions – with loyalty and work ethic defined by personal needs rather than organizational needs.

☑ Acknowledge their talents and expertise. Let them know that you can learn from them – and you're willing to do so.

☑ Use clear and specific language when communicating. Avoid corporate jargon, buzzwords, and clichés. Get right to the point (in a respectful manner) and don't sugarcoat bad news.

☑ Rely on technology (e-mail, voice mail, etc.) for much of your communication. Save meetings for issues that truly require face-to-face interaction.

☑ Remember that members of this group tend to place a high premium on efficiency – so don't waste their time. Do your best to minimize interruptions, avoid frivolous requests, and eliminate poorly organized activities.

☑ When it comes to how and when they accomplish assigned tasks, allow them as much flexibility and autonomy as is feasible and appropriate. Provide "freedom with fences." Establish the requirements and parameters – and let them operate within those boundaries as they see fit.

☑ Understand and honor their need for a balance between work and their personal lives. Better yet, help them achieve that balance whenever you can – as long as they are satisfactorily meeting all of the responsibilities and reasonable expectations that come with the job.

☑ Encourage, and contribute to, a friendly, open, and informal work environment. Use logic and reason, rather than power and authority, to direct their activities and behavior. Explain WHY you need them to do things and emphasize the personal benefits to be gained (What's in it for them).

My "Generation X" Coworkers
To Whom This Information Applies:
(write names in box)

Tips for Working Effectively With
"GENERATION Y"

SUMMARY OVERVIEW

Born between: 1982-2002

Motto: *Technology rules.*

History: Soon to be the largest group in the workforce, their history is still forming. They have grown up with multitasking, multimedia, and an unprecedented exposure to diversity, technology, violence, and sexual themes.

Characteristics: Generally seen as self-assured – with a global view. They tend to respond positively to opportunities involving technology.

☑ Acknowledge their talents and fresh perspectives. Let them know that you can learn from them – and you're willing to do so.

☑ Be open to, and accepting of, new and different (nontraditional) ways of working – as long as the job is getting done. Don't expect them to "fit your mold."

☑ Encourage and embrace technology. This is the cyber generation. They grew up (and are still growing) in a high-tech world. Because of their skills and knowledge in this arena, this group is a valuable resource for getting work done more efficiently. The more technology proficient *you* become, the easier it will be to work together.

☑ Create opportunities to involve them in projects of significance. Their diverse perspectives and technical knowledge can be invaluable to the success of your key business activities.

☑ Show that you respect them as important members of the team by soliciting their opinions or asking for their help.

☑ Offer to be a mentor – or to find one for them. Help them learn, develop, and grow – especially when it comes to the political, cultural, and interpersonal aspects of your organization. Provide them with frequent and timely feedback. Members of this generation ARE the workforce of the future that you need to help "groom."

☑ Keep your communications short, clear, direct, and specific. Avoid long-winded explanations. And periodically follow up to ensure that your message was understood.

☑ Do what you can to help build a fun, challenging, and fast-paced work environment. Look for ways to combine work and play.

My "Generation Y" Coworkers
To Whom This Information Applies:
(write names in box)

CLOSING THOUGHTS

Unquestionably, if the message of this book had to be distilled down to one word – to the single, most important key for working effectively with members of other generations – that word would be **RESPECT**.

Regardless of whether we do our work in person or electronically, each of us shares the responsibility of constantly looking for ways to be more considerate and respectful of others. Each of us must make a sincere effort to be less judgmental and more accepting. We all must avoid pointing fingers at others and labeling them "wrong," and instead pursue heightened levels of appreciation for our counterparts as contributing coworkers, unique individuals, and inherently valuable human beings. And that begins by pondering perhaps the most critical question of all:

What specifically am I doing to demonstrate respect for ALL of the people I work with ... and those I serve?

There's great truth in the old cliché "We're all in this together." Each of us is an important and somewhat differently shaped piece of a very large organizational puzzle. Our success as individuals is dependent on our collective ability to complete the puzzle.

And completing that puzzle ultimately is a matter of ...

generations working together.

"If It Wasn't For ..."

If it wasn't for TRADITIONALISTS, we wouldn't have ...

... the sage wisdom that only comes with age.

Nor the history to learn from as we enter each new stage.

We wouldn't see the loyalty so needed for success.

Nor the common sense we count on to avoid each pending mess.

Sure, their need to follow protocol may seem a bit too much,

but we none-the-less can count on them for a warm and human touch.

Thank goodness for these special folks who rarely search for fame.

If it wasn't for TRADITIONALISTS **we just wouldn't be the same.**

If it wasn't for BABY BOOMERS, we wouldn't have ...

... hard-working folks who don't go by the clock.

Nor the chance to pick the brains of those

who've "been around the block."

We wouldn't have the leaders who have made us what we are.

Nor their "can do" optimism that has taken us so far.

Perhaps it seems they have no lives and are often labeled fools,

yet the teamwork that they bring to us is the best of all our tools.

Thank goodness for these special folks who help us win the game.

If it wasn't for our BOOMERS **we just wouldn't be the same.**

If it wasn't for GENERATION X, we wouldn't have …

… so many perspectives that are new.

Nor the challenge to examine everything that we all do.

Without them only "nine to five" would be our way to go,

'cause we'd have much less incentive to step away from status quo.

While it seems their only interest is in doing things their way,

this group's focus on results has very often saved the day.

Thank goodness for these special folks who at times are hard to tame.

If it wasn't for our X-ERS **we just wouldn't be the same.**

If it wasn't for GENERATION Y, we wouldn't have …

… the growing push for workplace fun.

Nor the ability to quickly knock out work when under the proverbial gun.

There would be no fellow workers pushing all of us to see,

that everything can be improved with advanced technology.

Though we may not like that work for them is often just a "gig,"

the future that they represent is unquestionably big.

Thank goodness for these special folks who see older ways as lame.

If it wasn't for our GEN Y group **we just wouldn't be the same.**

If you truly want to be effective
in today's world, if you sincerely
want to understand other people,
it seems absolutely critical
that we accept the reality that
all these people out there who
are different from the way we are,
are just as RIGHT, CORRECT,
and NORMAL as us.

~ Morris Massey, Ph.D.